Introduction To Personal Branding

Introduction To Personal Branding

TEN STEPS TOWARD A NEW PROFESSIONAL YOU

Mel Carson

Table of Contents

Introduction

In July 2012, I was laid off from my role as Digital Marketing Evangelist at Microsoft. As the company streamlined its operations, a group of us learned our roles were eliminated. Microsoft was very good about it, of course, and offered to help us find other jobs within the company and externally. I felt positive about landing somewhere fresh and new after seven years in that position.

When I got back to my desk to contemplate my future, I wrote a blog post about the news to let people know that I was fine and was open to job offers.

The blog post went viral.

Over the next couple of days, major news publications mentioned my story and linked to the post. Ten thousand people read it, and the phone began ringing off the hook with companies wanting to hire me.

What struck me most about the blog post were the comments of support from people I had never even met. It turns out I'd built quite a brand in the digital marketing industry in the course of those seven years. While I knew many of those who followed me and would connect and engage with them online and at conferences, there were many, many more people who had come in contact with my writing, videos and presentations over the years but stayed silent until that point.

That's when the penny dropped and my company, Delightful Communications, was born out of my commitment to helping others consciously build their personal brand. Four years later, we've helped hundreds of people across the world make their wisdom and expertise discoverable, shareable and memorable.

This book is an edited compilation of articles I have written on the topic and is intended to help thousands more gain an understanding of the fundamentals of personal branding, with actionable tips to get the professional ball rolling in the direction you want it to go!

Take time to accomplish the ten steps in this book, and you'll begin establishing a personal brand that's approachable, endearing AND enduring. The next seven and a half thousand words have been designed to offer an introduction to the art of personal branding, rather than overwhelm with massive amounts of actions and to-do lists.

These tips are meant to inspire, with simple activities to help you see immediate results as you embark on your quest to stand out in your industry and create a career that you can be proud of.

If you have any questions at all, feel free to reach out to me via my website – MelCarson.com, and connect with me on LinkedIn and Twitter.

LinkedIn: https://www.linkedin.com/in/melcarson

Twitter: @MelCarson

And please consider leaving a review on Amazon, so we understand and celebrate the impact this book has had on your professional life and career.

CHAPTER 1

Establish Your Professional Purpose

Before you can tackle the creation of your perfect personal brand, it's important to understand who you are, what makes you tick and why you do what it is you do.

Simon Sinek's *How Great Leaders Inspire Action* TED Talk has been viewed over 22 million times online in large part because of his simple mantra: ***start with why.***

It's a powerful but often overlooked first step towards success in any area of life.

Nearly all of us have to work to pay the bills, pay off university loans, save into our pension funds, shrink the mortgage, go out on occasion, take vacations and hopefully have a bit of fun while we're not working.

If we know we have to work what might be a 40, 60, or even 80-hour week, there has to be more to what we're doing than just earning money. What helps us get out of bed in the morning? What helps us be better at what we do? What is it that separates a job from a career? How do we want to feel about our impact on the world in our twilight years?

We need more than a paycheck.

We need a professional purpose.

Without purpose, there can be no planning, and we limit the possibility of channeling our future in the direction we desire.

How I Discovered My Professional Purpose

My story started back in school when I realized I had a talent for acting, singing and writing. School plays, music festivals and talent shows all saw me pouring my heart and soul into something I knew I was good at. Drama at University was an obvious next step; the bright lights of London theater, TV, and film beckoned after three years of honing my craft.

I then spent six years selling teddy bears at Harrods and failing miserably at getting real acting jobs. I decided, at the age of 29, that I needed a new career. The Internet was pretty new, so I did a course in HTML and managed to conjure up an editor role at the search engine directory LookSmart.

My job involved writing 55 website reviews every day – short, punchy descriptions of what users might find if they clicked on a link. Soon after, I was promoted to traffic manager helping our European sales people get display ads live across the LookSmart network.

LookSmart folded in 2003, and I spent some time at a digital advertising agency before Microsoft came calling, and I spent the next seven years of my career working in an evangelism role. This meant more writing, speaking, video creation and other ways to communicate to an audience looking to be informed and inspired.

It was during those years I discovered what truly made me tick. My desire to act and write had little to do with being famous or earning loads and loads of money. What I really enjoyed – what got me out of bed in the morning – was the love of communicating, inspiring and educating people and businesses to do their very best work.

I wanted people to have a great experience.

I wanted to help people.

I wanted others to be successful.

And so my professional purpose was born:

To inspire and educate people and their businesses to be successful by applying digital marketing strategies that focus on Social Media, Digital PR and Personal Branding both online and in-person.

That's it.

Past Signposts Define Your Future Path

During my time helping executives and professionals with their personal brands, I've talked to some who aspired to be architects but now build successful businesses. I've met some who felt working with children was their calling, but they've turned out to be exceptional people managers or HR directors. And there are others who, while they were young, wanted to be engineers because they loved tinkering with things, but have now found successful careers as journalists, uncovering problems and making sense of the world for us through their detective work.

In order to establish your professional purpose, you need to look back at your early education and career and trace back the steps to where you are now.

Then consider these questions:

- Why is it that you do what you do?
- What thrills you about your current job role or career?
- Why don't you do something else?
- What does a great day look like?
- What does success look like beyond the paycheck?
- What does real success feel like for you?

- What is it you don't enjoy about your job and why?
- How do you want to feel about your impact on the world when you retire?

Answer those questions (and a few more of your own that you may uncover during the process), and you'll be well on your way to identifying and articulating your professional purpose.

Knowing why you do what you do and being able to succinctly articulate it is as crucial for your internal well-being and growth, as it is an external badge that makes up part of your personal brand.

Start with why and when you figure it out, I promise you, the answer will be far more satisfying than any paycheck.

CHAPTER 2

Embrace and Expound Your Experience

I have a story.

You have a story.

We ALL have a story.

Our personal brand is all about what kind of experience people have with us online and in-person, and that experience has a past. We need to embrace it.

During a personal branding workshop I delivered recently, we talked about our professional histories. What was our educational experience? How did we get into our niche? What were our professional passions? What did we find hard? Where did we want to be in three years' time from a career perspective?

In just five minutes talking about themselves (not an easy or comfortable thing for many to do), the participants had started to cultivate a story about their career that had structure – a beginning, middle and desired end.

When it comes to articulating your experience, it's important to set out your professional skills in a compelling way. Many people have an issue with writing down what, of all the experience they have in their career to date, is actually interesting or matters.

It all matters.

While embracing your experience and crafting a story you can succinctly articulate at a networking event or job interview is a goal, getting that information down in writing on your website or social platforms like LinkedIn is critical, as well.

Share Your Unique Value Propositions

When you're writing down your experience under present and past roles within your profile, include as much detail as you can. This means not just your job role, but expounding that experience with responsibilities, successes, awards, client names (if not confidential), and what value and impact you brought to the role.

Detail, detail, detail.

It's crucial to think about how people might be searching for you or your expertise. You don't have to write an essay, but share enough for people reading your profile or looking for your skillset to have a much more robust understanding of your past than a thin, buzzword-riddled, two-sentence rush job.

As I was talking through each of the fields on LinkedIn during the workshop, I had to stop people furiously editing their profile in real-time. I suggested they take time away from the workplace and jot experience down in a Word document before committing it to be published.

These things take time!

Hiding your light underneath a bushel does you no favors. Share the highlights and key accomplishments from your past professional experience. Your target audience is looking for you, but you're not providing them sufficient detail to figure out if you're the right person to answer their need.

If you're a procrastinator like me, take one job role at a time and write everything down you can remember. Then return to edit it down to salient points that help tell your story. This isn't something you can do in an hour or even a day.

You have a great story.

Start telling it more completely!

CHAPTER 3

Analyze Your Competitors as You Build Your Personal Brand

One of the biggest gaps I see companies unable to fill is the real-time understanding of what their competition is up to. During my years in digital marketing, I'll be the first to admit to being so down in the weeds executing on the tactical plan that I didn't have the wherewithal to notice what the competitive set was working on.

Having learned that lesson, one of the first things we do now is conduct a competitive analysis to see who's out there, what they are doing well and where the opportunities are to differentiate and stand out.

Competitive analysis is as important for you and your personal brand as it is for the company you work for.

Understanding what other people in your niche are doing, saying and how successful they are is vital to personal branding success. Here are a few things you can do to figure out who they are, their impact, and what you can do to wrestle attention away from them onto you.

Use LinkedIn to Research Your Industry

LinkedIn should be your first port of call. We use it to look for people with similar roles at similar businesses and see how well they are utilizing the platform. How well a person is using LinkedIn tells you a lot about how serious they are about their personal brand. Are they publishing content? How active are they on the platform, liking and commenting on other people's posts and updates? How robust is their profile? Have they filled out all the experience fields? Do they have a summary and, if so, how does it position them within your industry?

LinkedIn is a goldmine of competitive information to help understand who has what experience in your niche and how well they are engaging with their connections.

Your LinkedIn presence should be a living profile that you update on a weekly (even daily basis) because, in our experience, the number one blocker to anyone having a tip-top personal brand is time.

Make time to understand your competition on LinkedIn and make time to be engaging on a regular basis.

Mine Twitter for Like Minds

Use tools like Followerwonk, an influencer discovery tool like Traackr or a fantastic content sharing analysis tool like BuzzSumo to figure out who's influential in your field and study their footprint.

- How many followers do they have?
- What are they sharing?
- What's their social ratio (how much of what they share is personal versus professional)?
- What's their reach?
- What content seems to resonate best with their followers?

13

- Are they following as many people as are following them (always a good measure of authenticity in our opinion)?

Twitter is a great way to understand how others in your industry exude their personal brand in real-time. You can pick up tips from power users on what content you should be sharing and, more importantly, how agile and engaging you can be if you want to compete.

Stay Current on Where They Speak

An indicator of influence in any industry is being invited to speak at conferences and events. Scour the speaker pages of conferences to see who's speaking on subjects close to your area of expertise. Do a search for their name and the conference on Google or Bing to see if any journalist or blogger covered their session and read what was written about them.

Try and understand from their speech topics and extracts what their "angle" is and think of a way to differentiate or complement what they're focusing on if it's similar to your expertise. You don't want to give a conference organizer any reason to reject your speaking pitch, so make sure you know the lay of the land before you pitch a topic.

Remember: Quality Trumps Quantity, Always

While the beauty of digital and social media is the huge swathes of data it gives us, it's also important to measure quality and not get stuck on quantity. Combining a gut feel for the quality of the digital footprint your competitor may have with the amount of followers, engagement, content produced or shared, is far better than focusing on numbers alone.

Your number one goal by making your personal brand discoverable, shareable and memorable is to **instill trust** in anyone you engage with or are discovered by.

To quote Stephen R. Covey, author of the fantastic book The Speed of Trust:

> "Trust is equal parts character and competence... You can look at any

> *leadership failure, and it's always*
> *a failure of one or the other."*

Being competent enough to know what your competition is doing with their personal brand will help you set your character apart from theirs and limit the possibility of failure.

CHAPTER 4

Get a New Headshot – Your New Image Starts with an Image

One of the most overlooked (literally) tactics that will help build you a compelling personal brand is to get a new headshot.

As the saying goes, "a picture is worth a thousand words," so what thousand words (or handful) is your current LinkedIn profile picture or Twitter photo saying about you?

We can assimilate the information from an image 60,000 times quicker than the written word. That's why cat pictures and food photos get so much traction on Facebook. And let's not get started on the glories to be found on Pinterest and Instagram!

We love photos because they're easier to understand and quicker to fuel an emotion. Your job as guardian of your personal brand is to make sure your photo/headshot/avatar solicits a positive reaction, as it's often going to be the first thing people look at when perusing your social media profiles or reading your bio in a conference brochure.

Let's Look at the Facts

Images are crucial to the way we view the world. But when we drill further, we find that LinkedIn claims that social profiles on the site that have a headshot photo get 14 times more views. That's because when people are searching for you, or someone with your skillset, they are unlikely to click on a profile if it doesn't have a photo associated with it.

Having no photo obviously says something about you – maybe you're a bit lazy, you haven't put much thought into your profile, you're not really interested in creating the right impression, or you're technically inept and can't work out how to upload it.

That's fine! (Well it's not, really...)

On the other hand, what does having the WRONG kind of photo say about you?

Here are some of the photos I've seen on LinkedIn – using these as examples as LinkedIn is more for professional use – I'm not calling out individuals, but this is what I've seen photos of people doing recently:

- Playing golf.
- Watching sparklers burning on a cheesecake in a restaurant.
- Hanging off the side of a mountain upside-down.
- Cuddling a dog.
- Cycling in full helmet and sunglasses beaming by the Golden Gate Bridge.
- Eating a donut.
- Drinking beer or cocktails.
- Smoking.
- Showing off a tattoo!

Tips for Likeable Profile Images Backed by Research

In a fantastic study carried out by PhotoFeeler, where 800 profile photos were rated based on 60,000 ratings of "perceived competence, likability and influence," these were the recommendations:

- Don't wear sunglasses or block your eyes. Wearing a pair of shades makes you less likable, whereas having hair in your face will bring down your competence and influence levels.
- Squinting (or 'squinching' as they call it in their study results) apparently makes us seem more confident and comfortable. Wide eyes make us look terrified.
- SMILE!!! Looking happy and approachable was "by far the most impactful" characteristic.
- What you are wearing is a major factor too. Formal (suit and tie or business casual but not jeans and t-shirt) makes us look more competent and influential.
- Don't get too artistic. Cropped to head and shoulders (not zoomed in)

and simply edited (not Instagram-filtered) are the best approaches.

Invest in Your Personal Brand's Storefront

Many professionals need a new headshot. Something clean, professional and shows you care about the impression you make about yourself and the company you work for.

So let's scrap the cropped vacation photos, in a bar, at a wedding, at a black tie event, with your friend/wife/boyfriend's hand on your shoulder and invest in some nice photos of you that do your personal brand justice.

Getting professional headshots doesn't cost the earth. I got my shots done through a charity here in Seattle – Youth In Focus – and they cost $250.

What's $250 if it means you close more sales, get a new job with a 20% pay raise, get picked up by a national news show as an expert in your field, or simply look more trustworthy to someone you're about to meet in a professional capacity?

Your profile picture is your storefront. Do you want people to come in and find out more about you? Or are you happy for people to simply walk past without getting a real understanding of what you have to offer?

CHAPTER 5

How to Craft Your Personal Branding Statement

When we deliver our personal branding workshops and training, we have attendees work on a Personal Branding Statement.

This 3 step process starts with what we call "5 in 5" where we all sit down with a partner and each talks for five minutes about:

- Our educational experience
- Our work experience
- What we love about what we do
- What we find hard
- Where we want to be in 3 years' time

We use that information and our internal compass to define and establish a Professional Purpose – the reason why we do what we do and (beyond money) why we get out of bed in the morning.

These two steps combined help formulate a Personal Branding Statement that can be used as the basis for the all important LinkedIn summary which is so crucial for being discoverable and worth engaging on the platform.

There are a number of schools of thought on what should go into a Personal Branding Statement, but here are the three main elements we recommend:

- **What's Your Mission**? – The professional world has changed dramatically since the Internet came along. We have the opportunity to be bolder in our professional desires and take control of the direction we want to go. If you're satisfied with your Professional Purpose, use that to extrapolate a mission statement that gives anyone reading it no doubt where you want your career to head. Having a mission in the public domain acts as a sign post as well as a filter, and gives you something to feel accountable about.

- **What's Your Value?** – Your value comes in different shapes and sizes, so it's important to articulate it in multiple ways. Your experience, length of time in your industry, who you have worked for in the past, your educational background and what you're passionate about, all give an indication of your worth to a potential employer or client. It also indicates what you might expect in return for their patronage. Including some value indicators, both from your personal and your current businesses/company's perspective is an easy – but often overlooked – way of perfecting a more compelling personal brand.

- **Zero Hyperbole and Buzzwords** – Maybe it's my shy and retiring English sensibility, but I'm not a big fan of over-egging a Personal Branding Statement or LinkedIn summary with big, fancy, unsubstantiated and yawn worthy claims. Buzzwords are a no-no too. Here are the top ten according to LinkedIn:

Motivated, passionate, creative, driven, extensive experience, responsible, strategic, track record, organizational, expert

Take some time to craft a Personal Branding Statement that shows the real you intelligently and honestly, without seeming overblown and having a lack of self-awareness.

Here's mine as an example:

Focusing on helping businesses and individuals achieve success through enduring social media, digital PR and personal branding strategies, my 16 years online advertising industry experience and 7 years at Microsoft as their Digital Marketing Evangelist, enables me to provide counsel to my clients that is truly relevant, robust and real-time.

Always striving to keep pace with the ever-changing nature of digital media and technology, I aim to improve my client's' competitive position through partnership, tenacity, and accountability.

Notice I put the customer (my target audience) first, I mention the fields I work in and the valuable seven years I spent at Microsoft. I give an indication of the way I work and let anyone reading it be in no doubt about my mission.

It didn't take long to write, with maybe a day or so of editing, but it's a living statement. As my career reaches new milestones and other experience comes along that is of value, I'll adapt the statement accordingly.

As important as a Professional Purpose is to your internal professional self, a Personal Branding Statement is your shop front to the hundreds of people looking to hire, partner and connect with you.

During our Personal Branding Workshops, we have attendees write down everything they can think of that might be relevant in establishing their personal brand and then edit it based on peer feedback and attention to their mission, value, and experience.

Spend some time crafting it properly, and it will serve you until the day you retire!

CHAPTER 6

Make Your Personal Brand Discoverable

When we embark on an analysis of a client's digital footprint, one of the first things we look at is how discoverable they are across the web via search engines and social media. The ultimate goals of any successful personal brand exercise are to make you more discoverable, shareable and memorable, so discoverability is where we start.

Why?

Well, you might be the most knowledgeable person in your field, the go-to expert in your niche or have so much to say on a subject you're simply bursting to let the world know. If no one can find you, either by name or when looking for relevant information pertaining to your expertise, you may as well not exist.

Just over a year ago, a New York research consulting firm asked me to have a chat with a "digital marketing expert" who had a great idea for a startup and wanted to run it past me. We spent most of the 45-minute conversation talking about personal branding, and the fact that I could find no information online about him – his LinkedIn profile was a barren wasteland, and I could find nothing to corroborate the claim he was an expert in digital marketing. He understood this was a bad experience, especially if I had been a Venture Capitalist or journalist checking him out.

Sometimes you only get one chance with people. If your brand doesn't reflect substance and authenticity, that's bad. Not being discoverable is even worse.

Here are some ideas to help you get your brand in order, so you're more discoverable:

Use Your Real Name

At some point in your career, someone will be searching for you. It might be a recruiter or prospective employer, it could be a business contact you're about to meet for the first time, or maybe it's an industry peer you've known for years that has a potential lead for you (as happens to me regularly).

If you're serious about being discovered, make sure the social profiles and digital presence you care about, and across which you have nothing to hide, can be found under your real name.

Overhaul All Your Profiles

LinkedIn, Twitter, etc. all have profiles that are searchable either by Google or Bing or by the myriad different social media tools marketers and PR people use to discover influencers and experts to engage with.

I've talked about how to be discovered on LinkedIn in my Entrepreneur.com columns, but the key to being discoverable in search is to have a number of different profiles that rank for your name. Does your company have profile pages for employees? Have you spoken at a conference recently or written an article on a well-known blog or website recently?

Crosslink Your Profiles

Links from websites are hugely important in ranking sites for relevant keyword searches across the search engines. Our client Majestic.com is one of the go-to resources to understand both the quality and trustworthiness of sites that link to others on the internet, and we use it in personal branding audits to understand how influential someone might be based on their link profile.

It's important that you crosslink your social profiles so search engines can tell definitively that it's your LinkedIn or Twitter profile that should show up top and not someone else with the same name. My Entrepreneur.com profile is a good example of what I mean here.

The more links you can get, the more difficult it will be pushed off that top spot. There's a bit (actually a lot) more to SEO (search engine optimization), but that's it in a simple nutshell.

Put Yourself in Discovery's Way

This is where you start thinking laterally about how you can be discovered as having something to say, even if people don't know your name.

Here's a quick list:

- Intelligently and authentically commenting on blog posts or on Q&A sites, groups and forums like Quora or LinkedIn. Don't make it look desperate. Just be cool and share your thoughts by engaging in an empathetic way.
- Start a blog and maybe use your name as the blog site address to rank well. Populate the blog with posts pertaining to your niche so that people will find and associate you with that expertise. If you're worried about the time-suck of writing blogs posts, search for an article I wrote called: How to Write a Blog Post in 30 Minutes.
- Speak at conferences or seminars – we're spoiled in the digital marketing industry as there are many conferences and meet-ups we can try and speak at, but whatever your niche, there will be opportunities for you to share your knowledge from a podium somewhere in the

world. If you're smart, you'll optimize that speaking gig for maximum ROI by sharing your social channels and other digital properties at the start. People live-tweeting or writing about your session will link to you and share your wisdom beyond the people in the room.

These are just some ideas to get you on the road to your personal brand being more discoverable. Get in the groove of thinking like this, and it will become second nature. If you're serious about your career or business and you want to be known as someone to turn to for information or discourse, make yourself discoverable!

CHAPTER 7

How to Re-engineer Your Digital Presence

U p until now, much of the theory I have been explaining is designed to get you thinking about being more thoughtful and disciplined about how you present yourself both on and offline.

Now it's time for a checklist of more action-able tips you can use to get your digital presence optimized, so you're more dis-coverable, shareable and memorable:

Label Files with Keywords

This is a basic requirement that is often overlooked. For SEO purposes a file name can be an important factor in people be-ing able to discover you. So when you get a new headshot or want to upload a PDF or Word doc – ANYTHING – label it with keywords that people might use to search for you or your content.

All my photos are labeled mel-carson-delightful-communications.jpg which helps if people search for me or my company they see images related to me or my company in search engine results.

A social media white paper I wrote while at Microsoft ranked number one on Google for over five years partly because we labeled the file name: *social-media-white-paper-microsoft-advertising.pdf*, so it pays to spend a few seconds taking this extra step to ensure you try and rank properly for your name, company or expertise.

Update Your Social Profiles

Online profiles – especially on LinkedIn – should be seen as living testimonies to your professional life and experience – like the multimedia portfolio option you have to add images, presentations, and videos to your summary and experiences. An out of date presence on the web shows a certain amount of laziness, in my opinion, so getting up to speed and being disciplined about refreshing content on your profiles is hugely important, as you never know when someone is going to be looking for you or your expertise and needs to be impressed.

You wouldn't show up to work unkempt and casually out of date, so set aside time each month (at least) to go over your profiles and make sure the most current information and data is available for any potential connection.

Add Social Channels to All Touch Points

You'd be surprised how often I get out-of-office responders from people saying, "I'm out of the office until blah, blah, blah." They don't say where they are or what they're doing, they don't leave a link to their Twitter or LinkedIn profile for someone to click on and follow, they don't see the opportunity to leave a good impression about their personal brand at the same time as they're saying I'm not going to be able to respond to whatever you want anytime soon.

Out-of-office responders, email signatures, public presentations and business cards are all vehicles for your personal brand to hop aboard and be amplified through social signals.

Be Delightful

It goes without saying that in order for your audience/followers/fans to want to engage with you and whatever you have to say, you have to be authentic, useful, relevant and actionable.

The other tip I give people is that they need to be delightful. It's not just our company brand name; it's a word that brings with it a positive experience. The experience people have with your personal brand should be an engaging and enjoyable one.

Whenever we embark on a personal branding analysis and strategy recommendation for our clients, there's always a long list of tactics they need to consider becoming part of the daily routine.

In order to re-engineer your digital presence, these five tips are starters you need to infuse into your pro-active personal brand from now on *as a bare minimum* if you are not seeking additional profession-al help.

CHAPTER 8

Take 5 and Practice Writing

One stumbling block people looking to improve their personal brand come across is the fear of not having anything to say online. For whatever reason, they feel they are not interesting enough, or they are afraid to put themselves and their thoughts "out there."

At the other end of the spectrum, there are those who have no problem updating their social channels with a stream of consciousness devoid of actual thought or empathy for people they are hoping to reach.

In my opinion, the perfect personal brand is a balance between the two.

I've written articles about writing in the past like How to Write a Blog Post in 30 Minutes, 5 Twitter Tips That Will Enhance

Your Personal Brand and LinkedIn Buzzword List Revealed – Please Stop Using Them!

The main premise behind them is to encourage people to think before they share their thoughts online and to hone their writing skills over time.

To the people who fear they don't have anything interesting to say, we encourage them to get into the discipline of practicing their writing and really thinking about how to express themselves.

In my book, Pioneers of Digital, Google's digital marketing evangelist, Avinash Kaushik, talks about how he practiced writing his now hugely successful web analytics blog – Occam's Razor – on his wife and colleagues before unleashing it on the world.

My purpose in life would be to write a blog post that would meet three requirements that I formed for myself. It would be something incredible, relevant and of value. I formed this mantra, and then I practiced blogging for a month and a half where only my wife and my Intuit employees read the blog because I wanted to see that I could actually produce content that was incredible, relevant and of value. And it turns out I did, and I started a blog, and I was amazed that I got my first two comments.

He had a plan.

And although writing may come to him and others more easily than you or me, we all need to practice to be better.

Whether it's a 140 character update on Twitter or a 500-word post you want to share with the world on LinkedIn, take 5 minutes to really think about what you're writing. How might it resonate with the different connections you have across social networks and what action you want people to take when they finish reading your wisdom?

You don't want people reading your writing and thinking "so what?" because they may never return.

Making everything you write have a point takes practice.

Make time to take 5.

CHAPTER 9

How to Learn to Listen and Practice Empathy

One of the top requests we get at Delightful is from executives wanting to be seen as *thought leaders* in their field. They understandably want to build their personal brand around expertise, but during the analysis phase of the framework we design, there's often a huge gap between how often they communicate and how often they listen.

The biggest misconception when it comes to personal branding is that the focus should be all about you.

Yes, it's your personal brand we're trying to uncover and grow, but to make the best, most well-rounded impression on people in your sphere, you need to practice the art of listening and being empathetic.

Whether online or in-person, growing your network is important if you're going to amplify the message that you're a go-to person in your field for information or advice. Too often, though, you run the risk of showing up on social networks or at events with an agenda that smacks of self-interest and after a while that attitude wears thin and does not reflect well on you.

Professionals looking to position themselves in their industry need to strike a balance between talking about themselves and asking questions of others. It's human nature to talk about ourselves (especially in professional situations) because it makes us feel good. Whether we're happy about ourselves at that particular moment in time or not, it feels good to vocalize whatever is on our mind.

If it feels good for you, then it will feel good for other people, right? So make sure you take an interest and ask questions.

The Goal is to Instill Trust

Like any business, your goal is to build up trust with people you come into contact with that are (or might become) customers or business contacts. By asking questions, you're taking an interest, demonstrating empathy and showing you care. You're signaling loud and clear that you don't know everything (no one likes a know-it-all) and you are willing and open to new learning experiences.

It sounds so obvious, but you'd be surprised how many people in senior positions don't understand this simple concept applies to them as much as their business.

When it comes to empathy, we're talking about tweaking your listening skills, so you don't just hear what people are saying, but learn to understand from their perspective. This takes practice, but by asking more questions, you're creating a better lens through which to identify more closely what they are saying.

If every business needs to learn the art of listening and to be empathetic, then there's no reason why your personal brand can't reap similar benefits too.

So the next time you're on LinkedIn or Twitter make sure you're engaging and asking questions instead of just distributing your personal agenda. At the next conference or networking event you attend, try making a handful of people feel good by asking about them, their business, their successes, and concerns.

In order to have a well-rounded personal brand that makes the right impression, you need to strike a balance between what you know and what you have yet to learn.

Opening yourself up to curiosity and understanding might actually surprise you on your quest to quench the thirst generated by your professional purpose.

CHAPTER 10

Social By Design: Make Your Personal Brand Stand Out. Always.

In this final part, I want to encourage you to be "social by design."

I first heard the phrase from Carolyn Everson, my former boss at Microsoft Advertising and now Head of Global Advertising Solutions at Facebook. Adapted from the industry cry for brands to be "digital by design," Carolyn's morphing of the expression creates the perfect discipline for the busy professional of today.

Here are a few ideas of what it means to be "social by design":

Getting Your Social Infrastructure Right

I talk about it in detail in the post on How to Reengineer Your Digital Presence, but this is about making sure your social profiles – LinkedIn, Twitter, Facebook, Instagram, etc. – are set up properly, so you're half way to success. Your profiles need to be discoverable; they need to have the right security settings activated, and it needs to be easy for someone to interact with you, understand immediately what you are about, and share whatever you are trying to get out there.

Creating Great Content

This goes without saying, but if you're active on social and digital channels, you need to have something of value to say and learn to say it well. I've written about The Science of Great Content on LinkedIn before and an article on How to Write a Blog Post in 30 Minutes has been shared on Entrepreneur. com over 7000 times so take a look at those as inspiration for creating content in long and short form that your followers/audience are going to appreciate and share.

Optimizing Your Speaking Engagements

One of the best ways to get your ideas out into your industry is by pitching to speak at conferences within your niche. Too often people who have flown many miles to give a speech at a convention somewhere in the world limit the potential audience to just those in the room.

The trick they miss is adding social signals to their presentations that prompt delegates to share their onstage wisdom to their followers. Giving permission to Tweet and take photos is one way, but adding your handle and the event hashtag to the odd slide is another.

Sharing an easy to write down URL where they can get a copy of your presentation and connect with you would be the icing on the cake.

Be Social Even When Out of the Office

If you're traveling or on holiday, you'll probably set an "out of office" alert right?

That's a perfect vehicle for leaving someone with a good impression and picking up some connections on social media.

So don't just say, "I'm on vacation!" Tell people where you are and how they can follow your adventures by giving them a link to your Twitter or Instagram account. If you're speaking at a conference, link to a Twitter search for your handle and the conference hashtag so people can read what they are saying about your speech – assuming it went well!

Offer a Physical Trait People Can Remember

A couple of years ago, I wrote a post about the fact that business cards are not dead. I carry Moo cards that are large and thick. They stand out from others, and people always spend time complimenting me and asking where I got them. If you have business cards, remember to take them to meetings, networking events or conferences. There's nothing more awkward than having to do the "pocket pat" followed by some spurious story about leaving them in your hotel room.

Something physical is not limited to business cards either. Look sharp. Make an effort with your appearance in professional settings. Look to differentiate.

I always wear something that has red in it (shoes, shirt, handkerchief) as it's Delightful's color. Yours could be a color, some item of clothing or accessory. It sounds gimmicky, but it works. People need an icebreaker. Something physical can help start a conversation and make it memorable.

Don't. Ever. Stop.

One of the main objections I get from people who are reticent about embarking on an effort to get their personal brand shored up is a lack of time. If you've been through the ten steps of this Introduction to Personal Branding, you'll start seeing some improvements almost immediately.

Wholesale success takes time, though, sometimes months or years. Your professional profile needs to evolve, take shape and tell a story.

This is why when you start -- You. Can. Never. Ever. Stop.

CHAPTER 11

Update and Personal Branding Examples

Thanks very much for reading this updated version of my book. I hope it's inspired you to kick start your personal brand and take those first steps toward a new professional you that's more discoverable, shareable and memorable.

Over the last year since we published the original edition, my team at Delightful Communications and I have helped hundreds of people uncover and understand the power their personal brands can have, not just on their individual career, but also the companies where they work.

Leaders in HR, PR, and marketing are waking up to the fact that their people really are their best asset and are beginning to employ personal brand strategies and employee advocacy programs right through their organizations. A company-wide effort to encourage and grow people's careers where they play to their strengths and are encouraged to share their expertise and become useful within their industries makes for happy employees and a more outwardly trusted company.

We're are often asked who we think exude exemplary personal brands, so the team wrote an online article: *8 Amazing Personal Branding Examples You Can Learn From Today.* The post includes critiques of a whole bunch of inspiring people leading their companies with their personal brands like Jeff Weiner from LinkedIn, Chip & Joanna Gaines from HGTV, bestselling author Amy Cuddy, and, of course, Richard Branson from Virgin.

While your personal brand might not reach the level fame the people in our examples have achieved, they stand as beacons of authenticity and discipline you can learn from when it comes to making a better, more enduring impression on your niche.

Lastly, please take one minute to leave a review on Amazon/Kindle so we can gather valuable feedback as to the impact of the book and where we can improve for next time. At the time of writing we are proud to have just passed fifty five-star reviews. Keep that feedback coming!

If you've enjoyed the book, then please recommend it to your friends and sign up to our newsletter, The Delightful Times: http://dlghtfl.co/DelightfulTimes

If you have any questions or want to hire us to help take your personal brand to the next level and beyond, feel free to reach out to me via my personal website: MelCarson. com and at DelightfulCommunications. com and connect with me on LinkedIn and Twitter.

LinkedIn: https://www.linkedin.com/in/ melcarson

Twitter: @MelCarson

Mel Carson – Founder at Delightful Communications

Made in the USA
Middletown, DE
07 May 2017